SEO 2025: MUST-KNOW TECHNIQUES FOR EFFECTIVE SEARCH STRATEGIES

MICHAEL FINK

CONTENTS

INTRODUCTION

The world of search engine optimization (SEO) is constantly evolving. As we step into 2025, SEO is more critical than ever for businesses, marketers, and creators. The digital landscape has shifted dramatically over the past few years, with new technologies and user behaviors changing the way we approach online visibility. What worked in SEO five years ago is now outdated, and with the rapid pace of innovation, staying up-to-date has become not just important—but essential.

In this book, **SEO 2025: Must-Know Techniques for Effective Search Strategies**, we will explore the cutting-edge strategies and trends that are shaping the SEO world today. From the rise of AI and machine learning to the importance of user experience, we'll cover all the key factors that will influence SEO success in the years to come. Whether you're a seasoned SEO professional or just getting started, this book is designed to give you actionable insights to improve your search rankings and stay competitive in an increasingly digital-first world.

By the end of this book, you will have a solid understanding of the techniques that matter most for SEO in 2025, as well as a clear roadmap for optimizing your digital presence. Together, we will navigate through the complexities of search algorithms, user behavior, and content optimization to ensure you're equipped for the future of search.

CHAPTER 1: THE EVOLUTION OF SEO

Brief History of SEO

The story of SEO began in the 1990s when the internet was still in its infancy. Early search engines like Yahoo, AltaVista, and Ask Jeeves laid the foundation for what would become an essential element of digital marketing. Back then, search engines ranked websites based on simple criteria—how many times a keyword appeared on the page. It was an era of keyword stuffing and unsophisticated algorithms.

The launch of Google in 1998 marked a turning point in the history of search. Google introduced the PageRank algorithm, which revolutionized SEO by prioritizing the quality and quantity of links pointing to a webpage. This shift from keyword frequency to link-based authority laid the groundwork for more complex algorithms that would prioritize relevance, user intent, and content quality.

Over the years, Google's updates—Panda, Penguin, Hummingbird, and more—continued to refine the way search engines assess web content. The focus moved from simply matching keywords to understanding the meaning behind them, thanks to advances in natural language processing and semantic search.

1.2 The Major Shifts in SEO

SEO has seen significant transformations over the years. Here are some of the most impactful changes that have shaped the SEO landscape leading up to 2025:

1 **From Keywords to Search Intent:** The early days of SEO revolved around keyword optimization. However, as search engines evolved, they became better at understanding search intent—what users are looking for when they type in a query. This shift meant that instead of simply optimizing for specific keywords, businesses needed to create content that answered the broader needs of their audience.

2 **Rise of Mobile and Local SEO:** The mobile revolution changed how people search. With more users accessing the internet through smartphones, Google introduced mobile-first indexing in 2018, meaning that mobile-friendliness became a key ranking factor. Similarly, the growth of local search has made it essential for businesses to optimize for "near me" searches and focus on local SEO strategies.

3 **User Experience and Core Web Vitals:** In recent years, Google has placed a greater emphasis on user experience (UX). The introduction of Core Web Vitals—metrics that measure a site's loading speed, interactivity, and visual stability—has pushed SEO professionals to focus on technical optimization as much as content.

4 **Artificial Intelligence (AI) and Machine Learning:** Google's RankBrain, an AI-driven component of its search algorithm, has changed the game. RankBrain helps Google interpret complex queries and understand the nuances of human language. As we head into 2025, AI will only become

more integral to search, with algorithms learning from user behavior and improving over time.

5 E-A-T (Expertise, Authoritativeness, Trustworthiness): Quality content is no longer just about keywords and links; it's about building authority. Google's emphasis on E-A-T means that businesses need to establish credibility in their niche. Content from trusted sources, experts, and recognized authorities is rewarded with better rankings.

1.3 Algorithm Updates: Navigating Constant Change

One of the most challenging aspects of SEO is adapting to the regular algorithm updates from search engines, particularly Google. These updates can either help websites improve their rankings or send them plummeting down the search results. Over the years, some of the most significant algorithm updates include:

- **Panda (2011):** This update focused on content quality, penalizing sites with thin, duplicate, or low-quality content.
- **Penguin (2012):** Penguin targeted link schemes and spammy backlinks, putting an end to manipulative practices like buying low-quality links.
- **Hummingbird (2013):** A significant overhaul to Google's core algorithm, Hummingbird introduced semantic search, which focused on understanding the intent behind a search query rather than simply matching keywords.
- **Mobilegeddon (2015):** This update made mobile-friendliness a major ranking factor, prompting a shift toward responsive design and mobile optimization.
- **RankBrain (2015):** RankBrain is part of Google's machine learning algorithm, using AI to interpret and deliver search results based on intent and relevance rather than relying purely on keywords.
- **BERT (2019):** The Bidirectional Encoder Representa-

tions from Transformers (BERT) update enabled Google to better understand the context of words in search queries, improving the handling of natural language.

EACH OF THESE updates has transformed the way SEO is practiced. Today, SEO experts must stay agile, constantly monitoring changes and adjusting strategies to stay ahead. In 2025, the need for adaptability is greater than ever, as algorithms continue to grow more sophisticated with the integration of AI and machine learning.

1.4 Where We Are Now: SEO in 2025

As we move into 2025, SEO has become a complex interplay of technical expertise, content strategy, and user experience. Search engines are no longer just information retrieval systems; they are intelligent entities that understand human language, behavior, and intent. The days of "gaming the system" with keyword stuffing or link-building schemes are long gone.

In today's SEO landscape, success comes from understanding the needs of users and creating content that genuinely provides value. Search engines reward websites that offer fast, mobile-friendly experiences, authoritative content, and a seamless user journey. Businesses must now focus on user-centric optimization, combining technical prowess with strategic content marketing to thrive in this new era of search.

CHAPTER 2: CORE WEB VITALS AND USER EXPERIENCE

U nderstanding Core Web Vitals
In 2021, Google introduced Core Web Vitals as part of its page experience signals. These metrics focus on user experience and are now critical for SEO success. Core Web Vitals are made up of three key metrics:

1 **Largest Contentful Paint (LCP):** Measures how quickly the largest element on a page (like an image or block of text) loads. A good LCP score should be under 2.5 seconds.

2 **First Input Delay (FID):** Gauges the time it takes for a page to become interactive. A low FID score means users can start interacting with the page almost immediately after it loads (less than 100 milliseconds).

3 **Cumulative Layout Shift (CLS):** This metric assesses visual stability by measuring unexpected layout shifts. A good CLS score should be under 0.1 to ensure a smooth visual experience.

Optimizing these Core Web Vitals is essential, not just for better search rankings but for providing a better user experience. A slow, unresponsive, or visually unstable website can frustrate users and lead to higher bounce rates —ultimately impacting conversions and business success.

2.2 The Role of User Experience (UX) in SEO

Search engines like Google have increasingly emphasized the importance of user experience in their ranking algorithms. But what exactly does "user experience" mean in the context of SEO?

In simple terms, UX refers to how a user feels when navigating a website. Google's goal is to deliver the best possible results to its users, which means prioritizing websites that provide a seamless, enjoyable experience. Here's how UX factors into SEO in 2025:

1 **Page Speed:** Slow-loading pages are a major turn-off for users. Optimizing page speed is crucial to retaining visitors and reducing bounce rates. Tools like Google's Page-Speed Insights can help identify areas for improvement.

2 **Mobile Friendliness:** With the majority of searches now happening on mobile devices, having a mobile-responsive site is no longer optional—it's mandatory. Google's mobile-first indexing means that your mobile site's performance will directly impact your rankings.

3 **Navigation and Structure:** A well-organized, intuitive site structure helps users find what they're looking for quickly. Clear navigation, logical categories, and internal linking not only improve UX but also help search engines crawl and index your site effectively.

4 **Interactivity and Engagement:** Engaging users with interactive elements, such as quizzes, forms, or videos, can improve dwell time (the amount of time a user spends on a page). Higher dwell times are correlated with better rankings, as they signal to search engines that users find the content valuable.

5 Content Readability: Content that is easy to read and digest—both in terms of language and visual presentation—encourages users to stay longer on your site. Breaking up text with headings, bullet points, and images can make a huge difference in user engagement.

2.3 Practical Strategies for Optimizing Core Web Vitals

Now that we understand the importance of Core Web Vitals, let's look at some practical ways to improve them:

- **Improve LCP:** Reduce server response times, use efficient image formats like WebP, and compress large files. Lazy-loading images can also help by deferring the loading of off-screen images until the user scrolls down the page.

- **Enhance FID:** Minimize JavaScript execution time and reduce the amount of third-party scripts. A faster response time allows users to interact with your site sooner.

- **Reduce CLS:** Ensure that images and videos have defined dimensions to prevent layout shifts. Avoid inserting new content above existing content unless absolutely necessary.

By focusing on these areas, you can ensure that your website not only ranks better but also provides a positive experience for your users, increasing the likelihood of conversions and repeat visitors.

CHAPTER 3: SEARCH INTENT AND CONTENT OPTIMIZATION

The Rise of Search Intent

One of the most significant changes in SEO over the past few years is the increasing focus on search intent. Gone are the days when simply including the right keywords in your content was enough to secure top rankings. In 2025, search engines prioritize content that aligns with what the user is actually looking for—this is the essence of **search intent.**

At its core, search intent refers to the reason behind a user's query. Why did they search for a specific term? What are they hoping to achieve? Understanding and catering to the user's intent is crucial to creating content that not only ranks well but also satisfies the user.

Search intent can generally be broken down into four main types:

1 **Informational Intent**: The user is looking for information or answers to questions. For example, "What is SEO?" or "How does AI affect search rankings?"

2 **Navigational Intent**: The user wants to find a specific

website or page. An example would be typing "Facebook login" or "Amazon homepage."

3 Transactional Intent: The user is ready to make a purchase or perform a specific action. Search queries like "buy Nike shoes online" or "subscribe to Spotify" fit this category.

4 Commercial Investigation Intent: The user is researching products or services but hasn't made a purchase decision yet. Examples include "best smartphones 2025" or "top SEO tools for businesses."

By identifying the intent behind a search query, you can create content that directly meets the needs of your audience, increasing the chances of converting visitors into customers.

3.2 Optimizing Content for Search Intent

The key to ranking well in 2025 lies in creating content that matches the user's intent. Here's how you can optimize your content for each type of search intent:

1 Informational Content: When the intent is informational, your goal is to provide comprehensive, clear, and engaging content that answers the user's questions. For example, blog posts, how-to guides, and explainer videos work well for this type of intent. Focus on creating content that educates your audience while incorporating relevant keywords naturally.

2 Navigational Content: For navigational queries, it's crucial that your brand or website is easily accessible. Ensure that your website is well-optimized with internal linking, easy navigation, and clear branding. For instance, if a user is searching for "Nike store," having a strong, well-structured site with a dedicated store locator page can help.

3 Transactional Content: If the user has transactional intent, they are looking to make a purchase or take action.

Product pages, pricing details, call-to-action buttons, and easy-to-navigate checkout processes are vital. Make sure your content is optimized for conversions—include clear, compelling copy, customer reviews, and secure payment options.

4 Commercial Investigation Content: For users researching products or services, comparison guides, reviews, and case studies work best. Create in-depth content that helps users make informed decisions, and include data, testimonials, or demos that provide value. By offering trustworthy information, you can establish your brand as an authority and gain the trust of potential customers.

3.3 How to Identify Search Intent

Understanding search intent requires more than just looking at the keywords a user types into Google. You'll need to analyze the context and behavior behind the search queries. Here are a few methods to help identify search intent:

• **Analyze SERP Features:** The Search Engine Results Page (SERP) often gives clues about the intent behind a query. For example, if the SERP includes featured snippets or "People also ask" boxes, it's likely an informational query. On the other hand, if product listings or ads dominate the SERP, it's probably transactional.

• **Look at Query Phrases:** Certain words and phrases can indicate intent. Queries that include "how," "why," or "what" are usually informational, while words like "buy," "best," or "deal" suggest transactional or commercial intent.

• **Examine User Behavior:** Tools like Google Analytics and Search Console allow you to see which pages users are landing on and how they are interacting with your site. High bounce rates or short session durations may indicate a mismatch between the content you offer and the user's intent.

• **Leverage AI Tools:** AI-driven tools like SurferSEO or Clearscope can help you analyze search intent at scale by analyzing thousands of queries and revealing trends in search behavior. These tools allow you to optimize your content based on real-time data.

3.4 Crafting SEO-Friendly Content for 2025

In 2025, SEO-friendly content is not just about sprinkling keywords throughout your text—it's about aligning your content with user needs, intent, and experience. Here are a few strategies to ensure your content is optimized:

1 **Use a Topic Cluster Approach:** Instead of creating isolated pieces of content, organize your content into topic clusters. A central "pillar" page covers a broad topic, while related "cluster" pages dive deeper into subtopics. This structure not only helps with SEO but also improves navigation and user experience.

2 **Create Long-Form, In-Depth Content:** Studies show that long-form content tends to rank better in search engines. In 2025, content that is thorough and addresses all aspects of a topic is more likely to meet search intent and provide value. Aim for articles that are at least 1,500-2,000 words, depending on the topic.

3 **Optimize for Featured Snippets:** Featured snippets are prime real estate in search results, often appearing above the #1 ranking position. To optimize for snippets, structure your content in a way that answers specific questions concisely, using bullet points, lists, or tables where appropriate.

4 **Incorporate Semantic Keywords:** Google's algorithms have become more sophisticated in understanding related concepts and entities. Instead of focusing on exact match

keywords, use **semantic keywords**—words and phrases related to your main topic. This helps search engines better understand your content and match it to a wider range of queries.

5 Engage Users with Multimedia: In 2025, content is more than just text. Incorporating images, videos, infographics, and other multimedia elements not only enriches the user experience but also keeps visitors on your site longer, signaling to search engines that your content is valuable.

6 Focus on Readability: Make sure your content is easy to read and skimmable. Use short paragraphs, subheadings, and bullet points to break up large chunks of text. Tools like Hemingway or Yoast SEO can help assess the readability of your content and suggest improvements.

WITH A DEEP UNDERSTANDING of search intent, you can create content that not only ranks well but also resonates with your audience. In 2025, mastering the balance between intent, relevance, and user experience is crucial to SEO success.

CHAPTER 4: AI AND SEO IN 2025

The Role of Artificial Intelligence in Search
Artificial intelligence has become one of the most significant driving forces behind the evolution of SEO. In 2025, AI is not just a tool for advanced SEO professionals but a core element of search engine algorithms and user experiences. Google's RankBrain, BERT (Bidirectional Encoder Representations from Transformers), and other AI-driven systems have changed the way search engines interpret and rank content. Rather than relying solely on keywords and backlinks, AI now helps search engines understand the meaning and context behind search queries, delivering more relevant results to users.

AI is also transforming how marketers approach SEO. With AI, we now have tools that can analyze vast amounts of data, predict trends, and optimize content in real-time. This allows SEO strategies to be more dynamic, efficient, and user-focused.

4.2 RankBrain: Google's AI Learning Algorithm

One of the earliest and most impactful implementations of AI in search is Google's RankBrain. Introduced in 2015,

RankBrain is an AI-powered algorithm that helps Google process and understand search queries more effectively. While it started as a minor part of Google's overall algorithm, by 2025, RankBrain plays a pivotal role in determining search rankings.

RankBrain uses machine learning to interpret complex and ambiguous search queries, understanding the intent behind them rather than relying solely on keywords. It analyzes how users interact with search results, learning from their behavior to continually improve the accuracy of search results. For example, if users consistently click on a particular result for a certain query, RankBrain may elevate that result's ranking because it recognizes that it's highly relevant to the user's intent.

4.3 BERT: Understanding Context and Language

BERT (Bidirectional Encoder Representations from Transformers) is another groundbreaking AI technology that has revolutionized search. Launched by Google in 2019, BERT allows the search engine to better understand the context of words in a sentence, particularly for longer, conversational queries. Before BERT, Google's algorithms often struggled to interpret complex language or phrases that included multiple meanings. BERT, however, uses deep learning techniques to grasp the nuances of human language, enabling it to deliver more accurate and contextually relevant results.

For SEO professionals in 2025, optimizing for BERT means focusing on creating content that is clear, natural, and user-focused. Instead of over-optimizing content with repetitive keywords, SEO practitioners now need to ensure that their content addresses user questions and provides valuable, easily digestible information.

4.4 AI Tools for SEO in 2025

Artificial intelligence is not just transforming how search engines operate—it's also changing how SEO professionals work. A growing number of AI-powered tools are available in 2025 to help streamline and enhance SEO efforts. Here are some of the most important AI tools for modern SEO:

1 **Content Generation and Optimization Tools:** AI-driven tools like **SurferSEO, Frase,** and **Clearscope** analyze top-ranking pages for a given query and provide content recommendations. These tools help you understand which keywords, topics, and headings are most effective in ranking high on search engines. They also suggest improvements based on content structure, keyword usage, and readability.

2 **AI-Powered Keyword Research:** Tools like **Ahrefs, SEMrush,** and **Moz** use AI to analyze millions of search queries and suggest relevant keywords. These tools can predict keyword trends, reveal user intent behind search terms, and identify long-tail keywords that competitors may have overlooked.

3 **Automated Content Auditing:** AI tools such as **MarketMuse** and **ContentKing** can automatically audit your website's content, identifying areas for improvement. They use machine learning to assess factors like content quality, keyword usage, internal linking, and user engagement metrics, ensuring your site remains optimized for search engines.

4 **AI-Driven Analytics: Google Analytics 4 (GA4)** and other AI-powered analytics platforms provide deeper insights into user behavior. They use machine learning to identify trends, segment audiences, and predict user actions. In 2025, these tools offer highly personalized reports, helping businesses tailor their content and SEO strategies to meet specific user needs.

4.5 Personalization and Predictive Search

AI's ability to learn from user behavior has made personalized search experiences a reality. In 2025, search engines are highly individualized, delivering results based on a user's previous interactions, location, device, and preferences. This shift toward **personalization** means that two users searching for the same keyword may see different results based on their unique search history and behavior patterns.

Predictive search is another AI-driven innovation gaining traction in 2025. Predictive search uses machine learning to anticipate what a user is looking for before they finish typing their query. This feature is visible in tools like Google's autocomplete, where suggestions are offered as users type. Predictive algorithms also power smart assistants like Google Assistant and Siri, making search faster, more efficient, and more personalized.

For SEO professionals, this means understanding the user's journey and creating content that appeals to specific audience segments. To capitalize on personalized and predictive search, businesses need to focus on user experience, mobile optimization, and creating content that meets the diverse needs of their audience.

4.6 AI and Voice Search Optimization

AI is the driving force behind the rise of voice search, which has become a dominant search trend in 2025. Voice search, powered by smart speakers and virtual assistants, relies heavily on natural language processing (NLP) and machine learning to interpret spoken queries. By 2025, voice search accounts for a significant percentage of all searches, particularly on mobile devices and smart home assistants.

Optimizing for voice search requires a different approach than traditional text-based SEO. Voice search queries are typically longer, conversational, and more likely to be phrased as questions. Users tend to ask voice assistants questions like, "What's the best Italian restaurant near me?" or "How do I fix a leaky faucet?"

To succeed in voice search SEO, businesses should focus on:

- **Targeting Conversational Keywords**: Use natural language and question-based phrases that reflect how people speak. Instead of focusing on short, transactional keywords, prioritize long-tail keywords and conversational phrases that match voice search queries.

- **Structured Data and Featured Snippets**: Voice assistants often pull answers from **featured snippets**, so optimizing content for snippets is crucial. Structured data (Schema markup) can help search engines understand your content better and improve your chances of being featured in voice search results.

- **Local SEO**: Many voice searches are location-based, such as "Find a coffee shop near me." Ensuring that your business is optimized for **local SEO** (using Google My Business, local citations, etc.) can help you rank for these searches.

4.7 AI and the Future of SEO

As we move further into the future, AI will continue to transform the SEO landscape. Here are a few predictions for how AI will shape SEO beyond 2025:

- **Deeper Personalization**: AI will allow for even more personalized search experiences, using data from multiple devices and platforms to create highly tailored results. SEO will need to focus on crafting content that appeals to specific user groups and personalizing the user experience on-site.

- **Smarter Content Creation**: AI-powered content creation tools will become even more sophisticated, allowing for the automated generation of high-quality, relevant content. However, while AI can assist in creating content, the human touch—creativity, storytelling, and emotional connection—will remain vital for building authority and trust.

• **More Intelligent Search Algorithms:** Search algorithms will continue to evolve, becoming more intuitive and capable of understanding the context, intent, and nuances of user queries. SEO professionals will need to stay ahead of these changes by continuously adapting their strategies and focusing on providing real value to users.

CHAPTER 5: VOICE SEARCH AND CONVERSATIONAL SEO

The Growth of Voice Search

Voice search has seen explosive growth over the past decade, driven by advancements in AI, natural language processing (NLP), and the proliferation of smart devices. By 2025, voice search accounts for a significant percentage of all searches, particularly on mobile devices, smart speakers (like Amazon Echo and Google Home), and virtual assistants (such as Siri and Google Assistant). Voice search is fast, convenient, and allows users to interact with technology in a more natural, conversational way.

One of the main reasons for the rise of voice search is the increasing accuracy of speech recognition technologies. AI-powered systems can now understand and process complex voice queries with a high level of precision, making them more reliable and user-friendly. For businesses, this shift means adjusting SEO strategies to cater to spoken queries, which tend to be longer, more specific, and conversational compared to traditional text-based searches.

5.2 Differences Between Voice Search and Text-Based Search

Optimizing for voice search requires a different approach compared to text-based search. Here are some of the key differences:

1 **Conversational Queries:** Voice search queries are more conversational in tone. For example, instead of typing "best pizza restaurant NYC," a user might ask, "What's the best pizza restaurant in New York City?" These queries are often longer and more specific, reflecting how people speak in everyday conversations.

2 **Question-Based Queries:** Many voice searches are phrased as questions. Users tend to ask voice assistants for direct answers, such as "How do I change a flat tire?" or "What time does Starbucks close?" Optimizing for these types of questions means structuring your content to provide clear, concise answers.

3 **Intent and Local Search:** Voice search is often used to find local businesses or services. For instance, a user might ask, "Where's the nearest gas station?" or "Find a dentist near me." Optimizing for local SEO is critical for capturing voice search traffic, especially for businesses with a physical presence.

4 **Short Answers and Featured Snippets:** Voice assistants often pull answers from **featured snippets** or the **Position Zero** spot on Google. When users ask a question, the voice assistant reads back the snippet that appears at the top of the search results. This means that optimizing for snippets is key to succeeding in voice search.

5.3 Optimizing for Voice Search: Key Strategies

To rank well for voice search queries, businesses need to adopt a new set of SEO best practices. Here are the most important strategies for optimizing for voice search in 2025:

1 **Target Long-Tail, Conversational Keywords:** Since voice searches tend to be longer and more conversational, it's crucial to target long-tail keywords that mimic natural speech. Use keyword research tools like Ahrefs or SEMrush to identify common questions or phrases users might ask related to your industry. Incorporate these phrases naturally into your content, especially in headings and FAQs.

2 **Focus on Local SEO:** Many voice searches are location-based, so optimizing for local SEO is essential. Ensure that your business is properly listed in **Google My Business**, with accurate contact details, business hours, and location information. Including location-specific keywords and phrases (e.g., "near me," "in [city]") in your content can also help you rank higher for local voice searches.

3 **Optimize for Featured Snippets:** Voice search devices often pull answers from Google's featured snippets, so it's critical to optimize your content for this coveted spot. Structure your content in a way that answers common questions directly and concisely. Use bullet points, numbered lists, and tables to make your content easy for search engines to extract and display as a snippet.

4 **Create FAQ Pages:** FAQ (Frequently Asked Questions) pages are a great way to address common questions your audience might ask in a voice search. By creating comprehensive FAQ pages that include conversational, question-based queries, you increase your chances of ranking for voice searches. Organize your FAQs in a clear, easy-to-read format with direct answers to common queries.

5 **Optimize for Mobile:** Since a large portion of voice searches are conducted on mobile devices, optimizing your site for mobile is crucial. Ensure your website is fast, responsive, and provides a seamless user experience on mobile devices. Google's **mobile-first indexing** means that your

mobile site's performance will directly impact your rankings in both voice and text-based searches.

6 Improve Page Speed: Voice search users expect quick, accurate answers. If your website is slow to load, you risk losing potential visitors and hurting your rankings. Use tools like Google PageSpeed Insights to identify areas where you can improve page speed, such as optimizing images, reducing server response times, and minimizing JavaScript.

5.4 Structured Data and Schema Markup for Voice Search

Structured data plays a crucial role in helping search engines understand and categorize your content. By using **Schema markup**, you can provide search engines with additional context about your content, improving your chances of ranking for voice search queries.

For example, you can use structured data to mark up:

• **Business details:** Including your business name, address, phone number, and operating hours.

• **FAQs:** Marking up FAQ pages with the appropriate schema helps search engines pull questions and answers directly into search results.

• **Recipes, product reviews, or events:** If your site offers any of these types of content, structured data can help them appear in rich results, increasing visibility.

In 2025, structured data is more important than ever for helping search engines match your content to relevant voice search queries.

5.5 Optimizing for Voice Assistants and Smart Devices

As the popularity of virtual assistants and smart home devices grows, optimizing for these platforms is becoming increasingly important. Devices like **Amazon Alexa**, **Google Home**, and **Apple HomePod** are revolutionizing the way users interact with search engines. To optimize for these devices, businesses should focus on creating concise, voice-friendly content that answers common user queries.

Here are a few tips for optimizing for voice assistants:

• **Answer Direct Questions**: Voice assistants prioritize content that provides clear, direct answers to user questions. Focus on creating content that answers specific questions in a way that is easy to understand and concise.

• **Claim Your Google My Business Listing**: For local businesses, having an updated and fully optimized **Google My Business** listing is critical. Smart assistants often pull business information from Google's local listings, so ensuring your details are accurate and up to date will help you rank for location-based voice searches.

• **Use Natural Language**: Write your content in a conversational tone, similar to how people speak. Avoid overly technical or formal language, as voice assistants are more likely to pull content that mirrors natural speech patterns.

5.6 The Future of Voice Search and SEO

As AI continues to evolve, voice search will only grow more sophisticated. Here are a few predictions for how voice search will shape the future of SEO:

1 **Multimodal Search Experiences**: The future of search is not limited to voice or text alone. Multimodal search experiences, which combine voice, text, and visual elements, will become more common. For example, users might ask a voice assistant to search for a product and then receive visual results on their smart devices or smartphones. SEO strategies will need to adapt to cater to these diverse experiences.

2 **More Conversational AI**: Virtual assistants will continue to improve their conversational capabilities, offering more personalized and context-aware responses.

This means that SEO professionals will need to focus even more on creating content that aligns with user intent and answers specific questions clearly and accurately.

3 Voice Search for E-Commerce: As voice search becomes more integrated with e-commerce platforms, users will increasingly rely on voice assistants to make purchases. Optimizing product listings for voice search and creating easy-to-navigate shopping experiences will be key for businesses looking to capitalize on this trend.

4 Increased Emphasis on Local SEO: As more users turn to voice search for local queries (e.g., "Find a restaurant near me"), businesses will need to prioritize local SEO. Ensuring that your business is listed in local directories and has accurate information on Google My Business will be crucial for capturing local search traffic.

CHAPTER 6: THE FUTURE OF MOBILE SEO

Mobile-First Indexing: The Standard for SEO in 2025

In recent years, mobile-first indexing has become the default for Google's search rankings, and in 2025, this remains the standard for SEO. **Mobile-first indexing** means that Google predominantly uses the mobile version of a website for ranking and indexing purposes. If your site isn't optimized for mobile, it will negatively impact your search rankings, regardless of how well the desktop version is optimized.

As more people rely on their mobile devices for browsing and searching, mobile optimization has become non-negotiable for SEO success. Google continues to prioritize websites that offer seamless mobile experiences, and businesses must adopt a mobile-first mindset when designing their websites and creating content.

6.2 Mobile Search Behavior: Trends to Watch

User behavior on mobile devices differs from desktop, and understanding these differences is crucial for SEO strategies in 2025. Here are some of the key trends shaping mobile search behavior:

1 **On-the-Go Searches:** Mobile users are often searching for quick answers or immediate solutions while on the move. These searches tend to be action-oriented, such as looking for nearby businesses, making reservations, or finding directions. For SEO, this means optimizing content for **local search**, **quick answers**, and **mobile-friendly formats** that are easy to navigate on smaller screens.

2 **Voice Search Dominance:** As we discussed in Chapter 5, voice search is a growing trend, and mobile devices are one of the primary platforms for voice search queries. Optimizing for conversational, question-based queries and local search is crucial for capturing voice search traffic on mobile devices.

3 **Mobile E-Commerce: Mobile commerce** (or m-commerce) continues to rise in 2025, with more users making purchases directly from their smartphones. Mobile SEO strategies must prioritize optimizing product pages, enhancing mobile payment options, and creating seamless mobile shopping experiences. Sites that offer fast loading times, intuitive navigation, and easy checkout processes will gain a competitive edge in mobile search rankings.

4 **Short-Form and Visual Content:** Mobile users tend to consume content in shorter, more digestible formats. Short-form content, video, and visual elements such as infographics and images are highly engaging on mobile devices. In 2025, businesses that leverage multimedia content in their SEO strategies will be better positioned to capture and retain mobile users' attention.

6.3 Core Web Vitals: The Backbone of Mobile SEO

In 2025, **Core Web Vitals** are a critical ranking factor for mobile SEO. Google introduced Core Web Vitals in 2021 as a way to measure user experience based on three key metrics: **Loading (Largest Contentful Paint or LCP), Interactivity (First Input Delay or FID),** and **Visual Stability (Cumulative Layout Shift or CLS).** These metrics are used to evaluate how quickly a page loads, how responsive it is, and how visually stable it remains as it loads.

For mobile SEO, Core Web Vitals are especially important because mobile users expect fast, smooth experiences. Slow-loading pages or websites with poor interactivity will result in higher bounce rates and lower search rankings.

Here's how to optimize for Core Web Vitals on mobile:

• **Optimize Page Speed:** Use tools like **Google Page-Speed Insights** to assess and improve your site's loading time. Compress images, enable browser caching, and reduce the number of HTTP requests to ensure that your mobile site loads quickly.

• **Reduce Visual Shifts:** Avoid large layout shifts that disrupt the user experience. This can be done by properly defining the size of images and ads to prevent unexpected shifts as the page loads.

• **Minimize Input Delays:** Improve interactivity by ensuring that mobile users can engage with your content (e.g., tapping buttons, filling out forms) without experiencing delays. This involves optimizing JavaScript and reducing the time it takes for the browser to respond to user actions.

6.4 Mobile-Friendly Content: Best Practices

Creating content that's optimized for mobile devices involves more than just making it visually responsive—it also means tailoring your content to fit mobile users' preferences and behaviors. Here are some best practices for creating mobile-friendly content in 2025:

1 **Use Short Paragraphs and Sentences:** Mobile screens

are smaller, so breaking up text into short, readable chunks is essential for readability. Long paragraphs can overwhelm mobile users and increase bounce rates, so use concise sentences and paragraphs to make your content more scannable.

2 **Prioritize Visual and Interactive Content:** Mobile users are more likely to engage with visual and interactive elements, such as videos, images, and infographics. Incorporating rich media into your content not only improves engagement but also helps with SEO, as Google increasingly prioritizes multimedia content in search rankings.

3 **Implement Accelerated Mobile Pages (AMP): AMP** is a technology designed to make pages load faster on mobile devices by using streamlined HTML and limited JavaScript. While AMP is not a direct ranking factor, it can improve page load times and user experience, which are key elements in mobile SEO. AMP-optimized pages often rank higher in mobile search results, especially in competitive industries like news, e-commerce, and publishing.

4 **Optimize for Voice Search:** Since many mobile users rely on voice search, ensure that your content includes conversational, long-tail keywords. Providing clear and concise answers to common questions can help your site rank higher for voice queries on mobile devices.

5 **Design for Touch:** Mobile users navigate websites by tapping and swiping, so it's important to design a mobile-friendly interface that's easy to interact with. Buttons, links, and interactive elements should be large enough to tap comfortably, with enough space around them to avoid accidental clicks.

6 **Ensure Easy Navigation:** Navigation should be simple and intuitive on mobile devices. Use clear menus, breadcrumbs, and easy-to-find links to guide users through your

site. A good mobile experience encourages users to spend more time on your site, reducing bounce rates and improving SEO performance.

6.5 Mobile-First Content Creation Strategies

When creating content in 2025, adopting a **mobile-first approach** is key. This means designing and optimizing content specifically for mobile users, even before considering how it will look on desktop. Here are some mobile-first content creation strategies:

• **Use Responsive Design:** A **responsive website design** ensures that your content adapts seamlessly to different screen sizes and devices. Google prioritizes responsive websites in mobile search rankings, so ensuring that your site is fully responsive is critical for SEO success.

• **Focus on User Intent:** Mobile searches are often highly focused on solving immediate problems or finding specific information. Tailor your content to meet the needs of mobile users by providing actionable, solution-oriented information. Incorporate **FAQs**, **how-to guides**, and **step-by-step instructions** to address user intent effectively.

• **Leverage Micro-Moments:** Mobile users often search during **micro-moments**, which are brief, intent-driven actions that occur throughout the day (e.g., searching for a recipe while cooking, finding a nearby store while out shopping). To capture these micro-moments, ensure that your content is optimized to provide quick answers and relevant solutions in real-time.

6.6 The Future of Mobile Search: Predictions for 2025 and Beyond

As we look ahead, mobile search will continue to evolve, with several trends shaping the future of SEO beyond 2025:

1 **5G and Ultra-Fast Internet Speeds:** With the rollout of 5G networks, mobile users will experience even faster

internet speeds, making mobile search and browsing smoother and more seamless. Websites that can capitalize on these fast speeds with dynamic, engaging content will see higher engagement and better rankings.

2 Augmented Reality (AR) Search Experiences: Mobile devices equipped with augmented reality (AR) technology will offer new ways for users to interact with content and search results. In the future, users might use their phones to search for visual information in real-time, such as identifying a product by pointing their camera at it. AR search optimization could become a new frontier in SEO.

3 Deeper Integration of Voice and Visual Search: The convergence of voice and visual search technologies on mobile devices will create more multimodal search experiences. Users will be able to search by speaking a query or scanning an image with their phone, and SEO strategies will need to adapt to optimize for these diverse search methods.

4 Hyper-Personalization of Mobile Search Results: As AI and machine learning continue to advance, mobile search results will become even more personalized, offering users tailored content based on their location, preferences, and past behavior. SEO professionals will need to focus on delivering personalized experiences that match users' specific needs and contexts.

CHAPTER 7: CONTENT OPTIMIZATION AND USER EXPERIENCE IN 2025

The Changing Role of Content in SEO

In 2025, content is still king, but the definition of high-quality content has evolved. The days of keyword stuffing and focusing solely on search engines are long gone. Now, the success of a website depends on its ability to meet users' needs while still satisfying search engine algorithms. **User experience (UX)** and **content optimization** have merged into a single, cohesive strategy where delivering valuable, relevant, and engaging content is the cornerstone of SEO.

Content needs to serve three core purposes:

1 **Answer Users' Queries:** Whether a user is asking a question, looking for information, or seeking to complete a transaction, your content must offer clear, concise, and actionable answers.

2 **Engage and Retain Users:** Content must be engaging enough to keep users on your site, reduce bounce rates, and encourage deeper exploration of your pages.

3 **Satisfy Search Engines:** Content must be optimized

for search engines by incorporating relevant keywords, structured data, and technical SEO elements, all without compromising the user experience.

7.2 Content that Aligns with User Intent

In 2025, understanding **user intent** is critical to successful content optimization. Search engines are more sophisticated, using AI and machine learning to interpret user intent behind each query. Content must address the **four main types of search intent:**

• **Informational:** Users are looking for information or answers to questions. For example, "how to bake a cake" or "what is blockchain?"

• **Navigational:** Users are searching for a specific website or page. For example, "Facebook login" or "Amazon homepage."

• **Transactional:** Users are ready to make a purchase or complete a specific action. For example, "buy Nike shoes online" or "subscribe to Netflix."

• **Commercial Investigation:** Users are researching products or services before making a purchase. For example, "best smartphones 2025" or "iPhone 14 vs. Samsung Galaxy S22."

Content that aligns with user intent will not only rank better but will also result in higher engagement and conversions. Here's how to tailor your content to match different types of user intent:

• **Informational Content:** Create blog posts, articles, and how-to guides that provide detailed, authoritative information. Use headings and subheadings to structure the content for easy scanning.

• **Navigational Content:** Ensure that your brand's homepage, key product pages, and other high-priority pages are easily discoverable through search.

- **Transactional Content:** Optimize product pages with detailed descriptions, pricing, and easy-to-use CTAs (calls to action) to guide users toward making a purchase.

- **Commercial Investigation Content:** Develop comparison guides, product reviews, and case studies to help users make informed decisions.

7.3 The Role of User Experience (UX) in SEO

User experience has become an integral part of SEO in 2025. Search engines prioritize websites that offer smooth, intuitive, and enjoyable experiences for users. Metrics like **dwell time, bounce rate**, and **click-through rate (CTR)** directly affect rankings, making UX an essential part of any content strategy.

Here are the key elements of UX that impact SEO:

1 **Site Structure and Navigation:** A clear, logical site structure helps both users and search engines navigate your website easily. Use simple menus, breadcrumbs, and internal links to create a seamless user journey.

2 **Page Speed:** Slow-loading pages frustrate users and lead to higher bounce rates. Google continues to prioritize fast-loading websites in 2025, making page speed optimization critical. Compress images, enable caching, and minimize JavaScript to improve load times.

3 **Mobile-Friendliness:** As mobile usage continues to dominate, responsive design is essential. Websites that aren't mobile-friendly will struggle to rank well, as Google's mobile-first indexing favors sites that provide an optimal experience on mobile devices.

4 **Content Layout and Readability:** Content should be easy to read and engage with. Use short paragraphs, bullet points, and headers to break up text, and ensure that your font size and line spacing are suitable for both desktop and mobile users.

5 Interactive Elements: Interactive elements like quizzes, surveys, and calculators can enhance user engagement and increase time spent on the site. These elements also provide users with personalized experiences, helping to satisfy their intent more effectively.

6 Trust Signals and Security: Users are more likely to engage with websites they trust. Incorporating trust signals —such as HTTPS encryption, privacy policies, and social proof (like reviews and testimonials)—can boost credibility and SEO performance.

7.4 Optimizing for Search Engines and Users

In 2025, the balance between optimizing for search engines and providing value to users is more crucial than ever. Here are the key content optimization strategies that cater to both:

1 Keyword Optimization: While keyword stuffing is outdated, **keyword research** is still vital. Focus on long-tail keywords and conversational phrases that match user intent. Use tools like Ahrefs, SEMrush, and Google Keyword Planner to find relevant search terms and incorporate them naturally into your content.

2 Topic Clustering: Organizing content around **topic clusters** is an effective way to signal to search engines that your site is an authority on a specific subject. A topic cluster consists of a **pillar page** (which covers a broad topic in depth) and **cluster pages** (which focus on related subtopics and link back to the pillar page). This structure helps improve rankings for multiple related search terms while enhancing the user experience by providing comprehensive, well-organized content.

3 Schema Markup: Using **structured data** (Schema markup) helps search engines understand your content better, increasing the chances of appearing in rich results like **featured snippets**, **knowledge graphs**, and **carousels**. This improves visibility and click-through rates.

4 E-A-T Principles (Expertise, Authoritativeness, and Trustworthiness): Google's E-A-T guidelines emphasize the importance of high-quality, authoritative content. Content should be created by subject matter experts, thoroughly researched, and backed by credible sources. Including author bios, citations, and links to reputable websites can help boost your content's E-A-T.

5 Multimedia Content: Engaging multimedia—such as images, videos, podcasts, and infographics—enhances user experience and can improve SEO rankings. Search engines increasingly prioritize multimedia content that engages users and increases the time they spend on your site.

6 Internal Linking: A well-structured internal linking strategy helps users and search engines navigate your site. By linking to relevant content within your site, you create a web of connections that supports your overall SEO strategy while guiding users to explore more of your content.

7.5 Measuring Content Success: Key Metrics to Track

In 2025, tracking the right metrics is essential to measure the success of your content and UX strategies. Here are some of the key performance indicators (KPIs) to monitor:

1 Organic Traffic: The number of visitors coming to your site through search engines. A steady increase in organic traffic indicates that your SEO efforts are working.

2 Bounce Rate: The percentage of visitors who leave your site after viewing only one page. A high bounce rate may indicate that users aren't finding what they're looking for or that your content or UX needs improvement.

3 Time on Page (Dwell Time): How long users spend on

your site before leaving. Longer dwell times suggest that users are engaging with your content and finding it valuable.

4 Pages Per Session: The average number of pages users visit in a session. Higher numbers indicate that users are exploring your content in depth.

5 Conversion Rate: The percentage of visitors who take a desired action, such as signing up for a newsletter, making a purchase, or downloading a resource. Optimizing content for conversions can directly impact your business's bottom line.

6 Click-Through Rate (CTR): The percentage of users who click on your site from the search engine results page (SERP). Optimizing meta titles and descriptions to entice clicks is key to improving CTR.

7.6 The Future of Content and UX: What's Next?

As we look toward the future, here are a few trends that will shape content optimization and UX in the years to come:

1 AI-Generated Content: AI tools like GPT and other machine learning technologies are increasingly capable of generating human-like content. In 2025, these tools are being used to create personalized, scalable content at a rapid pace. However, AI-generated content must still be reviewed by humans to ensure quality and relevance.

2 Interactive and Immersive Experiences: Virtual and augmented reality (VR/AR) are becoming more integrated into content strategies. These technologies allow users to engage with content in new, immersive ways, offering opportunities for brands to create memorable, interactive experiences that enhance both UX and SEO.

3 Hyper-Personalization: As AI and data analytics

improve, content will become even more personalized, tailored to individual users based on their preferences, behavior, and location. Hyper-personalization will lead to higher engagement and conversion rates, as users receive content that's directly relevant to their needs.

CHAPTER 8: AI AND MACHINE LEARNING IN SEO

The Rise of AI in SEO

In 2025, artificial intelligence (AI) and machine learning (ML) have fully transformed the SEO landscape. Search engines like Google rely on complex AI-driven algorithms to process and rank vast amounts of data. SEO professionals need to adapt their strategies to work with these intelligent systems rather than against them. AI tools assist in automating processes, predicting trends, and delivering more personalized experiences to users, which ultimately leads to better search engine performance.

AI's role in SEO can be categorized into two main areas:

1 **Search Engine Algorithms:** Google's AI algorithms, particularly **RankBrain** and **BERT (Bidirectional Encoder Representations from Transformers)**, continue to evolve. These systems help Google better understand search queries, particularly those involving natural language and long-tail keywords, and improve how content is ranked.

2 **AI-Driven SEO Tools:** From content creation and keyword analysis to competitor research and trend predic-

tion, AI-powered tools like **Jasper, Surfer SEO**, and **Frase** help marketers optimize content more effectively and efficiently. AI tools are becoming indispensable for SEO professionals as they streamline workflows and provide data-driven insights.

8.2 RankBrain and BERT: Google's AI Powerhouses

RankBrain and **BERT** have fundamentally changed how Google processes search queries. Let's look at each in more detail and explore how they impact SEO in 2025.

RankBrain: Understanding User Intent

Google's **RankBrain** is an AI system introduced in 2015 that uses machine learning to better interpret and respond to complex queries. It analyzes search patterns to understand the context of queries rather than just matching keywords to results. By 2025, RankBrain has become more sophisticated, helping Google deliver search results that align with **user intent.**

To optimize for RankBrain:

• **Focus on User Intent:** As discussed in Chapter 7, aligning content with user intent (informational, transactional, navigational, or commercial investigation) is crucial. RankBrain rewards content that satisfies users' needs in context, rather than simply matching keywords.

• **Write Naturally:** RankBrain prioritizes content that mirrors natural human language. Instead of relying on awkward keyword placement, content should be conversational and readable, while still incorporating relevant phrases.

BERT: Enhancing Natural Language Processing

BERT, introduced by Google in 2019, represents a leap in natural language processing (NLP). It helps Google understand the full context of a word by looking at the words before and after it in a sentence. This advancement enables

Google to deliver more relevant search results, particularly for complex queries and questions.

SEO strategies in 2025 must consider BERT's ability to process conversational and long-tail keywords. Here's how to optimize for BERT:

• **Focus on Context:** Content must answer questions in clear, concise, and contextually rich ways. Google's BERT algorithm will reward content that doesn't just mention keywords but provides thorough, context-driven answers to user queries.

• **Optimize for Featured Snippets:** Featured snippets—those short, concise answers at the top of search results—are often powered by BERT. Content that provides direct, structured answers to questions is more likely to appear in these snippets, driving traffic and improving visibility.

8.3 AI in Content Creation and Optimization

AI-driven tools are revolutionizing content creation and optimization by automating many of the traditionally manual tasks involved in SEO. Here's how AI is shaping content strategies in 2025:

AI Content Generation

AI content generation tools like **Jasper, Copy.ai**, and **Writesonic** allow marketers to quickly generate human-like text. These tools are particularly useful for scaling content production, creating blog posts, product descriptions, and social media content at high volumes. However, while AI can assist in content creation, it's essential to review and refine AI-generated content to ensure quality, accuracy, and originality.

AI for Content Optimization

AI tools like **Surfer SEO**, **Frase**, and **Clearscope** analyze top-ranking pages and provide recommendations for optimizing content to rank better. These tools offer insights into:

- **Keyword Usage:** AI suggests keyword variations, LSI (Latent Semantic Indexing) terms, and related phrases to improve content relevance.

- **Content Structure:** AI can recommend the ideal structure for content, including headings, subheadings, and bullet points, to enhance readability and SEO performance.

- **Topic Clusters:** AI helps identify related topics and subtopics, allowing you to create **pillar content** and **topic clusters** that improve overall search visibility (discussed in Chapter 7).

Predictive Analytics

AI can predict future SEO trends by analyzing historical data and identifying patterns in search behavior. Predictive SEO tools help marketers stay ahead of the curve by forecasting shifts in search trends and suggesting new content ideas based on upcoming demand. This forward-thinking approach is invaluable in a rapidly changing SEO landscape.

8.4 AI for Personalization and User Experience

AI isn't just improving content creation; it's also enhancing the user experience. Personalized content is more engaging, and AI tools allow businesses to deliver tailored experiences to individual users, which improves user satisfaction and boosts SEO performance.

Dynamic Content Personalization

AI can track users' behavior, preferences, and search history to deliver personalized content. For example:

- **E-Commerce Sites:** AI algorithms recommend products based on users' past browsing and purchasing behavior, creating a highly personalized shopping experience.

- **Content Platforms:** AI-driven recommendation engines suggest related articles, videos, or tutorials to keep users engaged and on your site longer, which improves metrics like **time on site** and **bounce rate.**

Chatbots and Conversational AI

AI-powered chatbots are becoming increasingly popular as a way to enhance user experience. Chatbots can answer questions, guide users through a site, and offer personalized recommendations based on user queries—all while improving engagement metrics. Chatbots are especially effective for transactional websites, such as e-commerce platforms, where real-time assistance can lead to higher conversion rates.

8.5 The Future of AI in SEO: What to Expect Beyond 2025

AI will continue to evolve, shaping the future of SEO in ways we're only beginning to understand. Here are a few predictions for how AI and machine learning will influence SEO beyond 2025:

Hyper-Personalized Search Results

In the future, search results will become even more personalized, with AI considering an individual's search history, location, behavior, and preferences to deliver hyper-specific results. SEO professionals will need to focus on creating diverse content that appeals to different audience segments to remain relevant.

Voice and Visual Search Integration

As discussed in previous chapters, AI-driven voice and visual search will become more common, and optimizing content for these search methods will be critical. AI will continue to refine its ability to process voice commands and recognize images, pushing SEO strategies to adapt to these new search behaviors.

AI Content Moderation and Fact-Checking

As AI becomes more sophisticated, it may be used to

automatically moderate and fact-check content. This could reduce the spread of misinformation and ensure that only authoritative, trustworthy content ranks highly in search results. SEO professionals will need to prioritize accuracy and credibility in content creation to stay competitive.

Automation of Technical SEO

AI will likely automate many technical SEO tasks, such as crawl optimization, schema markup, and error detection. Tools like **DeepCrawl** and **Botify** already use AI to identify and fix SEO issues, and this trend will only accelerate, allowing SEO professionals to focus more on strategy and less on manual tasks.

CHAPTER 9: LOCAL SEO AND HYPER-TARGETED SEARCH STRATEGIES

The Importance of Local SEO in 2025

In an increasingly digital world, local SEO has become crucial for businesses looking to attract customers in specific geographical areas. With more users conducting **"near me"** searches and leveraging mobile devices to find local services, businesses must optimize their online presence to ensure they appear in local search results. In 2025, local SEO is not just about ranking well in search engines; it's about connecting with the community and delivering value to local consumers.

Key statistics underscore the importance of local SEO:

- **46% of all Google searches** are seeking local information.
- **76% of people** who search for something nearby visit a business within a day.
- **28% of those searches** result in a purchase.

This chapter will explore the best practices and strategies for optimizing local SEO and hyper-targeted search strategies in 2025.

9.2 Understanding Local Search Intent

Understanding **local search intent** is key to successful local SEO. Users conducting local searches often have specific intentions, such as finding directions, checking store hours, or making a purchase. The main types of local search intent include:

1 **Transactional Intent:** Users looking to make a purchase, such as "buy pizza near me" or "book a hotel in San Francisco."

2 **Navigational Intent:** Users searching for a specific business or location, such as "Starbucks near me" or "Walmart locations."

3 **Informational Intent:** Users seeking information about a local service or event, such as "best restaurants in Austin" or "upcoming concerts in my area."

To optimize for local search intent, businesses should ensure that their content clearly addresses these user needs. This can include creating location-specific landing pages, updating service area information, and providing relevant local content.

9.3 Google My Business (GMB) Optimization

One of the most significant tools for local SEO in 2025 is **Google My Business (GMB)**. Claiming and optimizing your GMB listing can significantly impact your visibility in local search results and Google Maps. Here are key elements to focus on:

1 **Complete Your Profile:** Ensure that your GMB profile is fully filled out, including your business name, address, phone number (NAP), website, hours of operation, and categories. Accurate information is vital for both users and search engines.

2 **Regular Updates:** Regularly update your listing with fresh content, such as posts about promotions, events, or

news. This engagement can help keep your listing active and relevant.

3 Encourage Reviews: Customer reviews play a crucial role in local SEO. Encourage satisfied customers to leave positive reviews, and respond to all reviews—positive or negative—to show that you value customer feedback.

4 Utilize Photos: High-quality images of your business, products, and services can enhance your listing. GMB allows businesses to upload various types of photos, including interior, exterior, and team images. Listings with photos receive **42% more requests for directions** and **35% more click-throughs to their websites.**

5 Add Posts and Q&A: Utilize the GMB posts feature to share updates and engage with your audience. Additionally, the Q&A section allows potential customers to ask questions about your business, and responding promptly can improve user engagement.

9.4 Local Keywords and Content Strategy

Incorporating local keywords into your SEO strategy is crucial for ranking well in local searches. Here's how to approach local keyword research and content creation:

1 Keyword Research: Use tools like **Google Keyword Planner**, **Ahrefs**, or **Moz** to identify local keywords that your target audience is searching for. Focus on long-tail keywords that include your location, such as "best coffee shop in Brooklyn" or "affordable plumbing services in San Diego."

2 Create Location-Specific Content: Develop blog posts, articles, and guides that cater to local interests and events. Content that highlights local attractions, provides tips for visitors, or discusses community news can help attract local traffic and improve your authority in the area.

3 Optimize On-Page SEO: Incorporate local keywords

naturally throughout your website, including in titles, headings, meta descriptions, and alt tags for images. Ensure that your NAP information is prominently displayed on your site.

4 Use Structured Data: Implement **schema markup** for local businesses to help search engines better understand your business information. This can enhance your chances of appearing in rich snippets and improving local visibility.

9.5 Building Local Citations and Backlinks

Building local citations and backlinks is essential for improving your local search visibility. Here are some strategies for enhancing your local SEO through citations and link-building:

1 Local Directories: Ensure your business is listed in local directories, such as **Yelp**, **Yellow Pages**, **Angie's List**, and niche-specific directories relevant to your industry. Consistency in NAP information across these listings is crucial.

2 Local Partnerships: Collaborate with other local businesses, community organizations, or influencers to build relationships and gain backlinks. Sponsoring local events, participating in community initiatives, or guest blogging on local websites can provide valuable link-building opportunities.

3 Engage on Social Media: Actively participate in local social media groups and communities. Share valuable content, engage with other local businesses, and promote your services. This can lead to organic backlinks and increased brand visibility.

4 Monitor Your Citations: Use tools like **Moz Local** or **BrightLocal** to monitor your local citations, ensuring accuracy and consistency across platforms. Address any discrepancies promptly.

9.6 The Role of Mobile Optimization in Local SEO

With the rise of mobile searches, optimizing your website for mobile devices is essential for local SEO. Key mobile optimization strategies include:

1 **Responsive Design:** Ensure your website is mobile-friendly and provides a seamless experience across devices. A responsive design automatically adjusts to fit the screen size, improving usability and user experience.

2 **Fast Loading Times:** Mobile users expect quick loading times. Optimize images, reduce server response times, and leverage browser caching to improve page speed on mobile devices.

3 **Local Intent Features:** Implement features that cater to mobile users, such as click-to-call buttons, location maps, and easy-to-navigate menus. These features enhance user experience and encourage conversions.

4 **Optimize for Voice Search:** With the increase in voice-activated search, optimize for voice queries by focusing on natural language and local phrases. Users often ask questions in a conversational manner when using voice search, so your content should reflect this.

9.7 Measuring Local SEO Success

Measuring the success of your local SEO efforts involves tracking key metrics that indicate performance and engagement. Here are some essential KPIs to monitor:

1 **Local Organic Traffic:** Monitor the number of visitors arriving at your website from local search results. Use tools like **Google Analytics** to track traffic sources.

2 **Google My Business Insights:** Utilize GMB insights to analyze user engagement with your listing. Metrics such as searches, views, and actions taken (calls, directions, visits) provide valuable data on how well your GMB listing performs.

3 Ranking for Local Keywords: Regularly track your rankings for targeted local keywords. Tools like **SEMrush** or **Ahrefs** can help you monitor keyword performance and identify opportunities for improvement.

4 Customer Reviews and Ratings: Monitor the number and quality of reviews on your GMB profile and other platforms. Increased positive reviews can lead to higher trust and visibility in local searches.

5 Conversions and Leads: Track the number of conversions generated from local search traffic, whether that's calls, online bookings, or in-store visits. Measuring these conversions can help evaluate the effectiveness of your local SEO efforts.

9.8 The Future of Local SEO: Trends to Watch

As we move beyond 2025, several trends are likely to shape the future of local SEO:

1 Increased Focus on Hyper-Local Targeting: Businesses will need to tailor their marketing efforts to increasingly localized audiences. This means focusing on niche communities and even smaller geographical areas to stand out in a competitive market.

2 Augmented Reality (AR) Integration: As AR technology advances, businesses may use it to enhance the customer experience and drive foot traffic. For example, a retail store could provide AR navigation to guide users directly to its location.

3 More Emphasis on Voice Search: As voice search continues to grow, optimizing for voice queries will be essential. Businesses must adapt their content to answer questions conversationally and succinctly.

4 Local Video Marketing: Video content will play a more prominent role in local SEO strategies. Creating engaging videos that showcase local products, services, or community involvement can enhance brand visibility and engagement.

5 AI-Powered Local Recommendations: AI will increasingly help deliver personalized local recommendations based on users' preferences, behaviors, and locations. Businesses must adapt their strategies to align with these AI-driven changes in search behavior.

CHAPTER 10: SEO ANALYTICS AND PERFORMANCE MEASUREMENT

The Importance of SEO Analytics

In the fast-paced world of digital marketing, understanding the effectiveness of your SEO strategies is critical for success. **SEO analytics** enables you to measure, analyze, and improve your online performance, guiding your efforts to ensure that your website is visible, relevant, and engaging to users. As we move into 2025, the ability to leverage data-driven insights for SEO optimization has never been more vital.

Key benefits of SEO analytics include:

• **Identifying Trends:** Understanding user behavior and search trends helps you adapt your strategy to meet evolving demands.

• **Measuring ROI:** By tracking conversions and traffic sources, you can measure the return on investment for your SEO efforts.

• **Optimizing Strategies:** Regularly reviewing your analytics enables you to identify areas for improvement and refine your SEO tactics accordingly.

10.2 Key SEO Metrics to Track

To effectively measure SEO performance, focus on the following key metrics:

1 Organic Traffic: This metric tracks the number of visitors arriving at your site through unpaid search results. Tools like **Google Analytics** can provide insights into overall traffic and traffic from specific keywords or landing pages.

2 Keyword Rankings: Monitoring your rankings for targeted keywords is essential for assessing the effectiveness of your SEO strategy. Tools like **SEMrush**, **Ahrefs**, and **Moz** can help you track keyword performance over time.

3 Click-Through Rate (CTR): CTR measures the percentage of users who click on your link after seeing it in search results. A higher CTR indicates that your title tags and meta descriptions are compelling and relevant to user queries.

4 Bounce Rate: Bounce rate tracks the percentage of visitors who leave your site after viewing only one page. A high bounce rate may indicate that your content is not engaging or that users are not finding what they expected.

5 Conversion Rate: This metric measures the percentage of visitors who complete a desired action (e.g., making a purchase, filling out a form, or signing up for a newsletter). Understanding conversion rates helps you evaluate the effectiveness of your content and user experience.

6 Backlink Profile: Monitoring your backlink profile is crucial for assessing your site's authority and credibility. Tools like **Majestic** and **Ahrefs** can help you track the quantity and quality of backlinks to your site.

7 Page Load Speed: Website speed is a ranking factor and impacts user experience. Use tools like **Google PageSpeed Insights** or **GTmetrix** to assess and optimize your site's loading times.

10.3 Using Google Analytics for SEO

Google Analytics is a powerful tool for tracking and analyzing SEO performance. To make the most of Google Analytics, focus on the following features:

1 **Acquisition Reports**: These reports provide insights into where your traffic is coming from, allowing you to see how much of your traffic is organic. You can also analyze which keywords are driving the most traffic to your site.

2 **Behavior Reports**: These reports offer insights into how users interact with your site, including which pages are most popular, average session duration, and bounce rates. Understanding user behavior helps you identify areas for improvement.

3 **Conversion Tracking**: Set up goals to track specific actions users take on your site, such as completing a purchase or signing up for a newsletter. This allows you to measure the effectiveness of your SEO efforts in driving conversions.

4 **Custom Dashboards**: Create custom dashboards to monitor key metrics relevant to your SEO strategy. This enables you to focus on the data that matters most to your business and track performance at a glance.

10.4 Utilizing Google Search Console for SEO Insights

Google Search Console (GSC) is another essential tool for monitoring your website's performance in Google search results. Key features include:

1 **Performance Reports**: These reports show how your site performs in search results, including total clicks, impressions, average CTR, and average position for specific queries. This data helps you understand which keywords are driving traffic.

2 **Index Coverage**: GSC provides insights into how well Google crawls and indexes your site. You can identify issues

that may prevent your pages from ranking well, such as crawl errors or indexing problems.

3 **URL Inspection Tool:** This tool allows you to check how Google sees a specific page on your site. You can see if the page is indexed, any crawl errors, and how the page performs in search results.

4 **Mobile Usability:** GSC highlights any mobile usability issues, ensuring your site provides a positive experience for mobile users. With the increasing number of mobile searches, addressing these issues is essential.

10.5 A/B Testing for SEO Optimization

A/B testing is a method for comparing two versions of a webpage to determine which performs better in terms of user engagement and conversion rates. Here's how to effectively implement A/B testing for SEO:

1 **Identify Test Elements:** Focus on specific elements to test, such as headlines, images, call-to-action buttons, or layout. Keep the tests limited to one variable at a time for clear results.

2 **Define Success Metrics:** Establish clear success metrics, such as increased CTR, reduced bounce rate, or higher conversion rates. This will help you evaluate the effectiveness of each version.

3 **Run Tests:** Use tools like **Google Optimize** or **Optimizely** to run your A/B tests. Ensure that you have a large enough sample size for statistically significant results.

4 **Analyze Results:** Review the data to determine which version performed better based on your success metrics. Implement the winning variation and consider testing other elements to continue improving your site.

10.6 Integrating SEO Analytics with Other Marketing Efforts

SEO doesn't operate in isolation; it's crucial to integrate

your SEO analytics with other digital marketing efforts for a comprehensive view of performance. Here's how to achieve this:

1 **Combine SEO with Content Marketing**: Track the performance of your content marketing campaigns alongside your SEO metrics. Analyze which types of content drive traffic and conversions, and adjust your strategy accordingly.

2 **Sync SEO with Social Media**: Monitor how social media efforts influence your organic search performance. Track referral traffic from social media platforms and identify trends in user engagement.

3 **Align SEO with PPC Campaigns**: Understand how your SEO efforts complement your paid advertising campaigns. Analyze which keywords drive organic traffic and consider leveraging those insights in your PPC strategy.

10.7 The Future of SEO Analytics

Looking ahead, SEO analytics will continue to evolve, with emerging trends shaping how we measure success. Here are a few key developments to watch for:

1 **Increased Use of AI and Machine Learning**: AI-driven analytics tools will enhance the ability to predict trends and automate reporting. These tools will help marketers identify actionable insights more quickly and efficiently.

2 **Real-Time Data Monitoring**: As technology advances, real-time data monitoring will become more common, enabling marketers to respond to trends and changes immediately.

3 **Greater Emphasis on User Experience Metrics**: Search engines increasingly prioritize user experience signals, such as page load speed and mobile usability. Monitoring these metrics will be essential for maintaining visibility in search results.

4 **Integration of Voice Search Analytics**: As voice

search continues to grow, analytics tools will evolve to track and measure voice search performance, enabling businesses to optimize their strategies accordingly.

5 Predictive Analytics: The use of predictive analytics will help marketers anticipate changes in search behavior, enabling proactive adjustments to SEO strategies.

CHAPTER 11: THE FUTURE OF SEO: EMERGING TRENDS AND TECHNOLOGIES

Introduction to Future Trends in SEO

As the digital landscape evolves, so too does the practice of search engine optimization (SEO). The future of SEO is not just about ranking high on search engine results pages (SERPs); it involves understanding user intent, leveraging new technologies, and adapting to ever-changing algorithms. In this chapter, we will explore the emerging trends and technologies that will shape the future of SEO and discuss how businesses can prepare for these changes.

11.2 The Rise of AI and Machine Learning in SEO

Artificial intelligence (AI) and machine learning are revolutionizing SEO practices by enabling search engines to deliver more personalized and relevant results to users. Here are some ways AI is transforming SEO:

1 **Improved Search Algorithms:** Search engines like Google increasingly rely on AI algorithms, such as Rank-Brain and BERT, to understand user queries better. These algorithms analyze vast amounts of data to identify patterns and provide more accurate search results.

2 Content Generation: AI-powered tools can assist in content creation by generating topic ideas, suggesting keywords, and even writing articles. This technology can help marketers streamline their content strategies and produce high-quality content more efficiently.

3 Voice Search Optimization: As voice search technology improves, AI plays a crucial role in understanding natural language queries. Optimizing for voice search will require businesses to focus on conversational keywords and phrases.

4 User Behavior Analysis: AI can analyze user behavior to predict trends and preferences, enabling businesses to create more targeted and personalized content. This insight can inform SEO strategies and enhance user engagement.

11.3 The Growing Importance of User Experience (UX)

User experience (UX) has become a critical factor in SEO success. Search engines are increasingly prioritizing websites that provide a positive user experience. Key aspects of UX that will impact SEO in the future include:

1 Core Web Vitals: Google has introduced Core Web Vitals as ranking signals, focusing on user experience metrics such as loading performance, interactivity, and visual stability. Businesses must optimize their websites to meet these standards to maintain visibility in search results.

2 Mobile-First Indexing: With the majority of searches now conducted on mobile devices, Google has transitioned to mobile-first indexing. This means that Google primarily uses the mobile version of a site for indexing and ranking. Businesses must ensure their websites are mobile-friendly to improve user experience and SEO performance.

3 Visual and Interactive Content: As users seek more engaging content, incorporating visuals, videos, and interactive elements can enhance the overall user experience.

Websites that provide a rich, multimedia experience are more likely to keep users engaged and reduce bounce rates.

11.4 The Evolution of Search Intent and Semantic Search

Understanding search intent is paramount for SEO success. The future of SEO will place even greater emphasis on semantic search and user intent. Here's how businesses can adapt:

1 **Focusing on Topic Clusters:** Instead of targeting individual keywords, businesses should create content around broader topics. This involves developing pillar content and interlinking related articles to provide comprehensive coverage of a subject.

2 **Optimizing for Natural Language Processing (NLP):** Search engines are increasingly using NLP to understand user queries. Businesses should focus on creating content that addresses common questions and uses natural language to align with user intent.

3 **Long-Tail Keywords:** As users become more specific in their searches, optimizing for long-tail keywords will become increasingly important. These keywords often reflect a clear intent and can drive highly targeted traffic.

11.5 The Impact of Voice Search on SEO

Voice search continues to grow, driven by the popularity of virtual assistants like Siri, Alexa, and Google Assistant. Businesses must adapt their SEO strategies to accommodate this trend:

1 **Conversational Keywords:** Optimize content for natural language and conversational queries. Users are more likely to ask questions in a casual tone when using voice search, so targeting these phrases can improve visibility.

2 **Featured Snippets and Position Zero:** Securing a

featured snippet position (often referred to as "Position Zero") is crucial for voice search optimization. Focus on providing concise, clear answers to common questions to increase your chances of being featured.

3 Local Search Optimization: Voice search often includes local queries, such as "Where is the nearest coffee shop?" Businesses should ensure their local SEO strategies are robust, including optimizing Google My Business listings and local citations.

11.6 The Role of Visual Search in SEO

Visual search technology is becoming increasingly sophisticated, allowing users to search using images instead of text. As visual search grows, businesses must adapt their SEO strategies accordingly:

1 Image Optimization: Optimize images by using descriptive filenames, alt text, and proper sizing to improve visibility in image search results. High-quality images can enhance user engagement and attract more visitors.

2 Visual Content Strategy: Incorporate visual content, such as infographics and videos, into your content strategy. This can improve user experience and increase the likelihood of shares and backlinks.

3 Schema Markup for Visual Content: Implement schema markup for images and videos to help search engines understand the content better. This can enhance your chances of appearing in rich snippets and visual search results.

11.7 The Future of Link Building

Link building remains a cornerstone of SEO, but the strategies for acquiring backlinks are evolving. The future of link building will focus on quality over quantity:

1 Emphasis on Authority and Trustworthiness: Links from authoritative and trustworthy websites will carry more weight in the future. Businesses should focus on building relationships with reputable sources in their industry to acquire high-quality backlinks.

2 Content Marketing and Outreach: Creating valuable content that attracts links organically will become increasingly important. Additionally, proactive outreach to industry influencers and journalists can help secure mentions and backlinks.

3 Diversification of Link Sources: Businesses should diversify their link-building efforts by seeking links from various sources, including social media, online communities, and local directories. This helps create a more natural backlink profile.

II.8 Preparing for the Future of SEO

To stay ahead of the curve, businesses should take proactive steps to prepare for the future of SEO:

1 Stay Informed: Keep up with the latest SEO trends and algorithm updates. Follow reputable SEO blogs, attend industry conferences, and participate in webinars to stay informed.

2 Invest in Technology: Leverage emerging technologies, such as AI-powered tools and analytics platforms, to enhance your SEO strategies and improve efficiency.

3 Focus on User-Centric Strategies: Always prioritize the user experience in your SEO efforts. Creating valuable, relevant content and providing a seamless user experience will position your business for success in the future.

4 Adapt and Experiment: SEO is constantly evolving, so be prepared to adapt your strategies based on performance data and industry changes. Experiment with new techniques and stay open to innovative approaches.

CHAPTER 12: CONCLUSION: THE PATH FORWARD IN SEO

Reflecting on SEO Evolution

As we reach the conclusion of this book, it's important to reflect on the evolution of search engine optimization and consider the trends and insights discussed throughout the chapters. SEO has transformed significantly over the years, moving from simple keyword stuffing to a multifaceted approach that prioritizes user experience, high-quality content, and technical precision.

The emergence of new technologies, such as AI, machine learning, and voice search, has reshaped how businesses approach SEO, making it more essential than ever to stay informed and adaptable. As search engines become increasingly sophisticated, so must our strategies.

12.2 Embracing Change and Innovation

In the ever-evolving landscape of SEO, embracing change is crucial. As we look ahead, businesses must remain agile and open to new ideas and methods. The following strategies will help ensure that your SEO efforts remain effective and relevant:

1 **Continuous Learning:** The digital marketing land-

scape is dynamic, and ongoing education is vital. Invest in training for yourself and your team to keep up with the latest developments in SEO and related fields.

2 Data-Driven Decision Making: Leverage analytics to guide your SEO strategies. Use data to understand user behavior, track performance metrics, and refine your approach for maximum impact.

3 Testing and Iteration: Adopt a mindset of experimentation. Regularly test different tactics, from content formats to user engagement strategies, to identify what resonates best with your audience.

4 Collaboration Across Teams: SEO is no longer the sole responsibility of one department. Collaborate with content creators, social media managers, and web developers to create a cohesive and effective digital marketing strategy.

12.3 The Importance of User-Centric SEO

At the heart of effective SEO lies a commitment to understanding and meeting user needs. As search engines evolve, they increasingly prioritize user experience and satisfaction. To succeed in this environment, consider the following:

1 Focus on Quality Content: Create content that provides real value to users. Answer their questions, solve their problems, and offer insights that establish your authority in your niche.

2 Optimize for User Experience: Ensure that your website is user-friendly, mobile-responsive, and accessible. A seamless experience will lead to higher engagement and conversion rates.

3 Build Community and Engagement: Foster a sense of community around your brand. Encourage user interaction through comments, social media, and email newsletters to build relationships and loyalty.

12.4 Preparing for Future Challenges

As the digital landscape continues to shift, businesses must prepare for emerging challenges. Here are some key considerations for the future:

1 **Algorithm Updates:** Stay vigilant and be ready to adapt to algorithm changes. Regularly monitor industry news and updates from search engines to adjust your strategies as needed.

2 **Increased Competition:** As more businesses recognize the importance of SEO, competition will intensify. Focus on differentiation through unique value propositions and specialized content.

3 **Regulatory Changes:** Be aware of potential regulatory changes regarding data privacy, advertising, and search practices. Stay informed to ensure compliance and adapt your strategies accordingly.

12.5 The Future of SEO: A Call to Action

The future of SEO is bright but requires commitment, creativity, and a willingness to embrace change. As you move forward, consider the following actions:

1 **Develop a Comprehensive SEO Strategy:** Ensure your strategy encompasses technical SEO, content creation, link building, and analytics. A holistic approach will yield the best results.

2 **Leverage Emerging Technologies:** Explore how AI, machine learning, and automation can enhance your SEO efforts. Invest in tools that streamline processes and provide actionable insights.

3 **Commit to a User-Centric Approach:** Always prioritize the user in your SEO efforts. Understand their needs,

preferences, and behaviors to create content and experiences that resonate.

4 Stay Agile and Adaptable: The SEO landscape is ever-changing, and your strategies must evolve accordingly. Be prepared to pivot your approach based on performance data and industry trends.

12.6 Conclusion: Your SEO Journey Begins

As we conclude this journey through the landscape of SEO in 2025, it is essential to remember that SEO is not a one-time task but a continuous journey. The strategies and techniques outlined in this book are merely the beginning. Your commitment to learning, adapting, and innovating will ultimately determine your success in the digital marketplace.

With the right mindset and a proactive approach, you can navigate the challenges and opportunities of SEO, ensuring that your business remains visible, relevant, and successful in the years to come. Embrace the future, and let your SEO efforts drive you toward new heights of success.